WILD EARTH

HURRICANES!

BY MARCIE ABOFF

ILLUSTRATED BY ALEKSANDAR SOTIROVSKI

Consultant: Susan L. Cutter, PhD
Director, Hazards and Vulnerability Research Institute
Department of Geography
University of South Carolina
Columbia, South Carolina

CAPSTONE PRESS
a capstone imprint

First Graphics are published by Capstone Press,
1710 Roe Crest Drive, North Mankato, Minnesota 56003.
www.capstonepub.com

Books published by Capstone Press are manufactured with paper
containing at least 10 percent post-consumer waste.

Library of Congress Cataloging-in-Publication Data
Aboff, Marcie.
 Hurricanes! / by Marcie Aboff ; illustrated by Aleksandar Sotirovski.
    p. cm.—(First graphics. Wild earth)
 Includes bibliographical references and index.
 Summary: "In graphic novel format, text, and illustrations explain how
hurricanes form, how they are named and measured, and how to stay safe
during one"—Provided by publisher.
 ISBN 978-1-4296-7607-6 (library binding)
 ISBN 978-1-4296-7951-0 (paperback)
 1. Hurricanes—Juvenile literature. I. Sotirovski, Aleksandar, ill. II. Title. III.
Series.
 QC944.2.A25 2012
 551.55′2—dc23
                                                          2011028741

Editorial Credits
Christopher Harbo, editor; Juliette Peters, designer;
    Nathan Gassman, art director; Kathy McColley,
    production specialist

Printed in the United States of America in Stevens Point, Wisconsin.
102011   006404WZS12

Table of Contents

A Hurricane Is Coming

Out in the ocean, a storm is spinning.

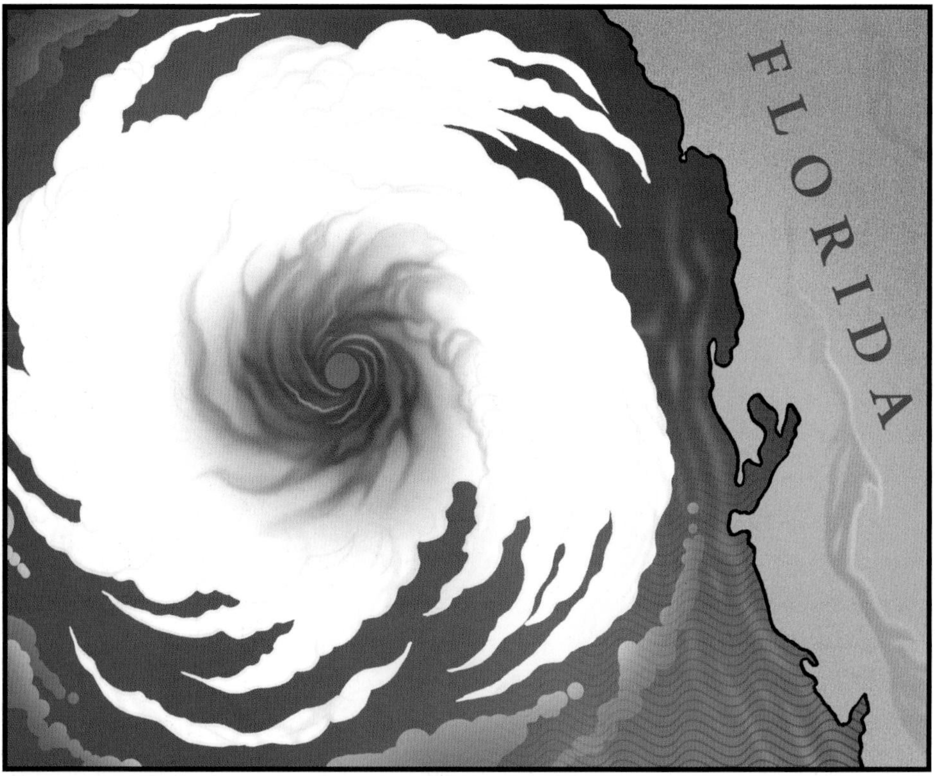
FLORIDA

As it hits land, strong winds bend trees.

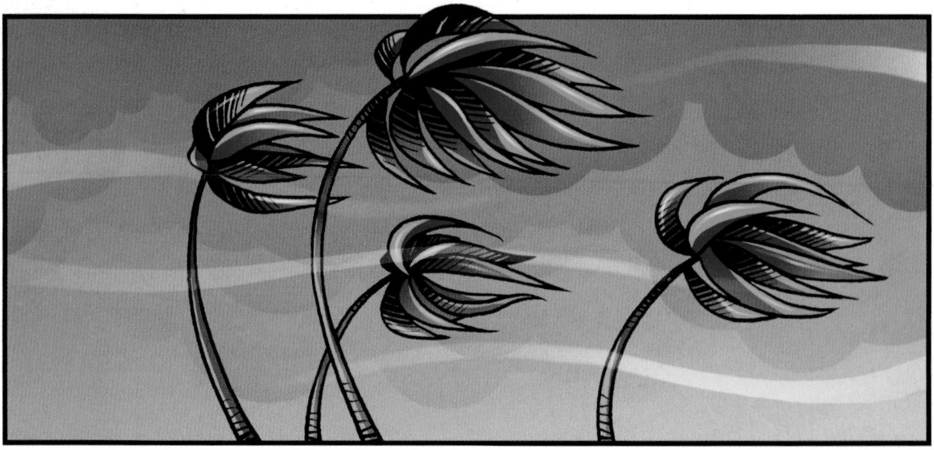

Huge waves pound beaches.

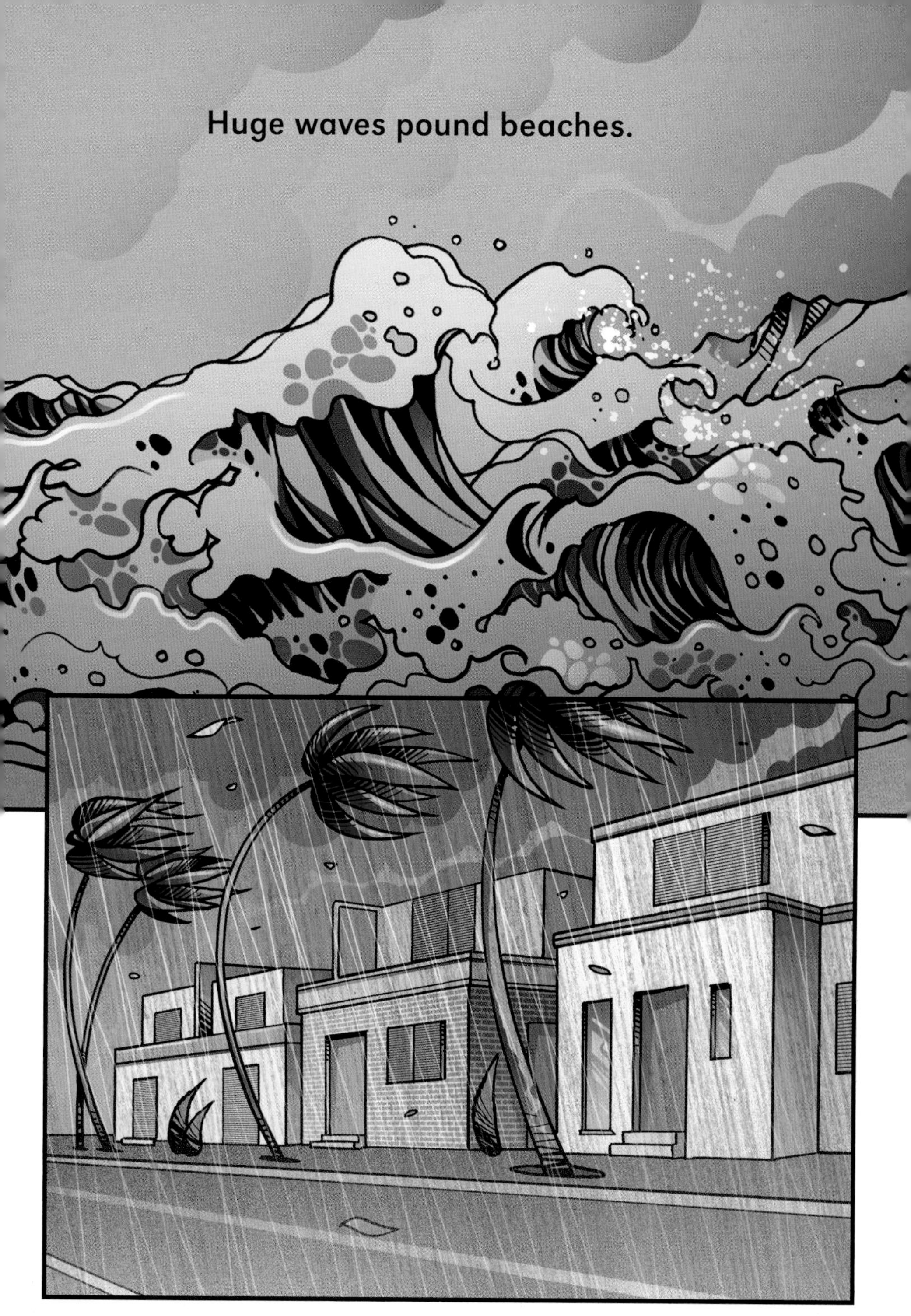

Sheets of rain pour from the clouds. A hurricane has come to shore.

Hurricanes are powerful storms that form over warm, tropical ocean water.

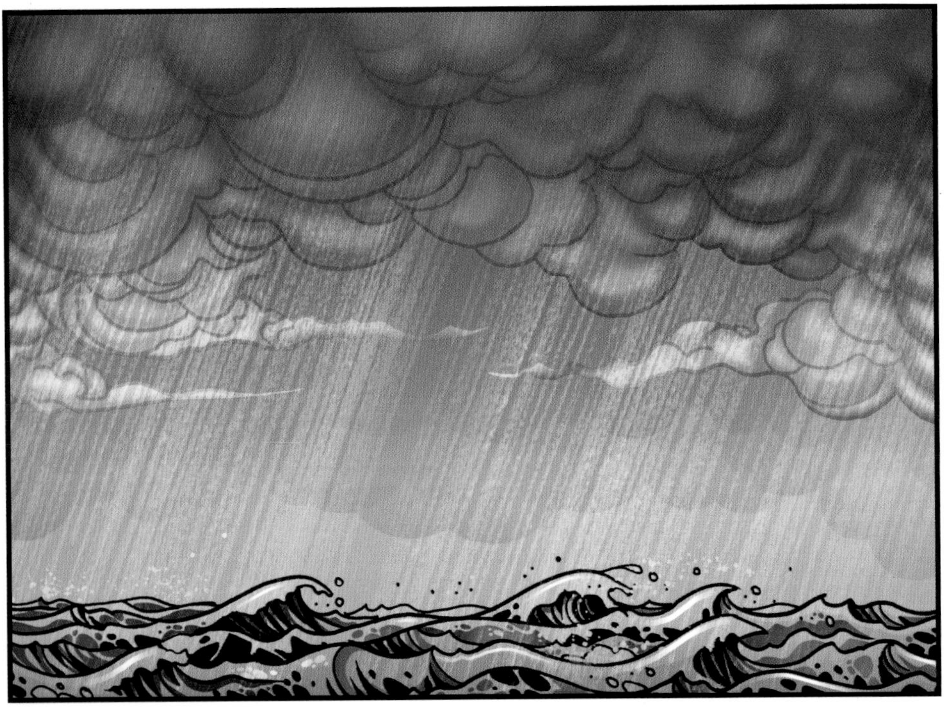

Warm, wet air rises into the sky.

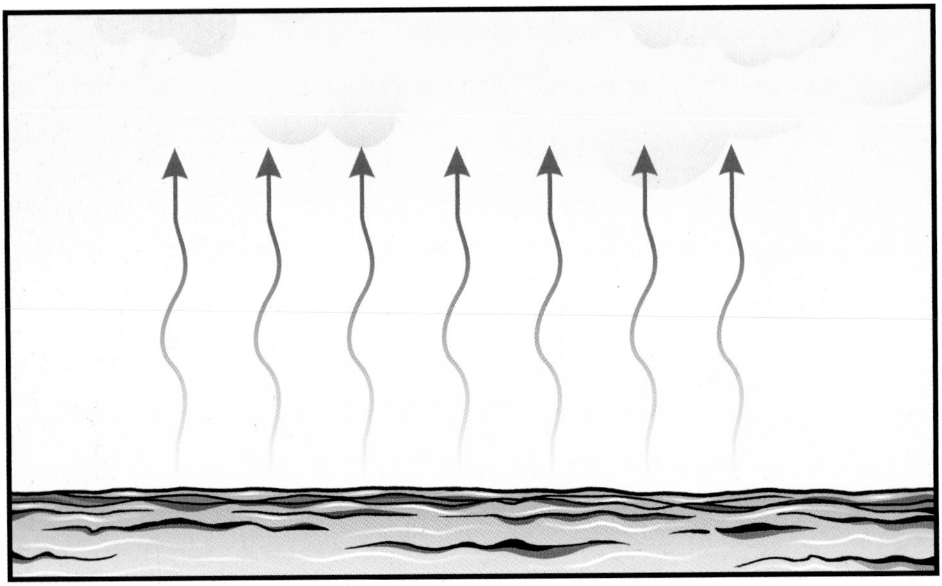

The wet air forms clouds and thunderstorms.

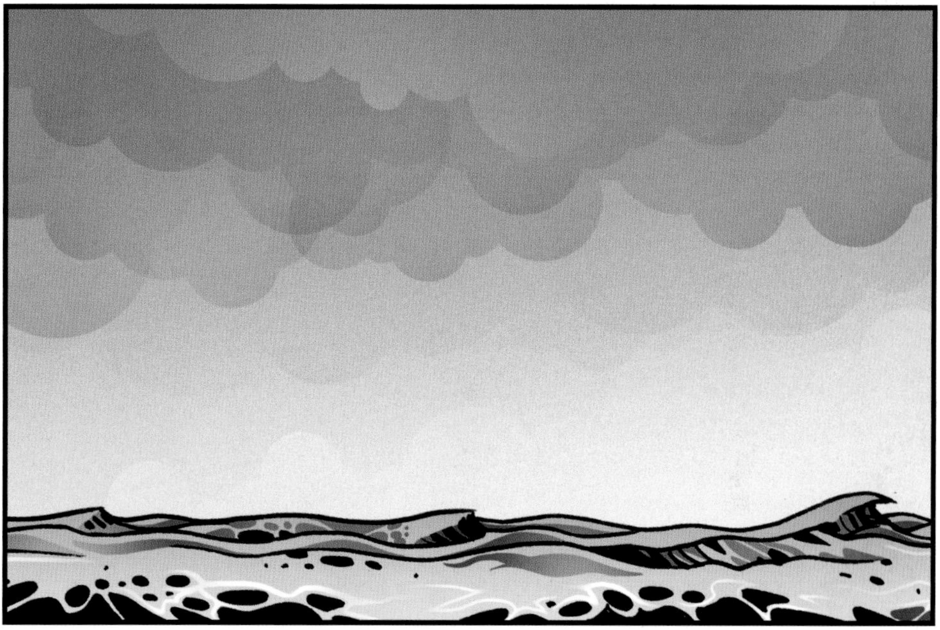

Thunderstorms gather together in a spinning circle to form a hurricane.

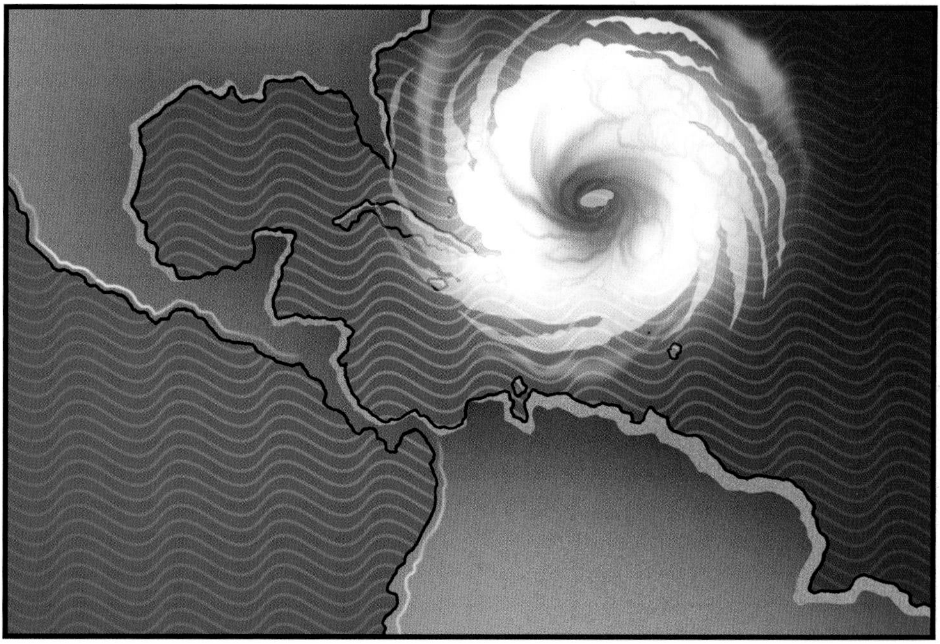

A hurricane is shaped like a doughnut.

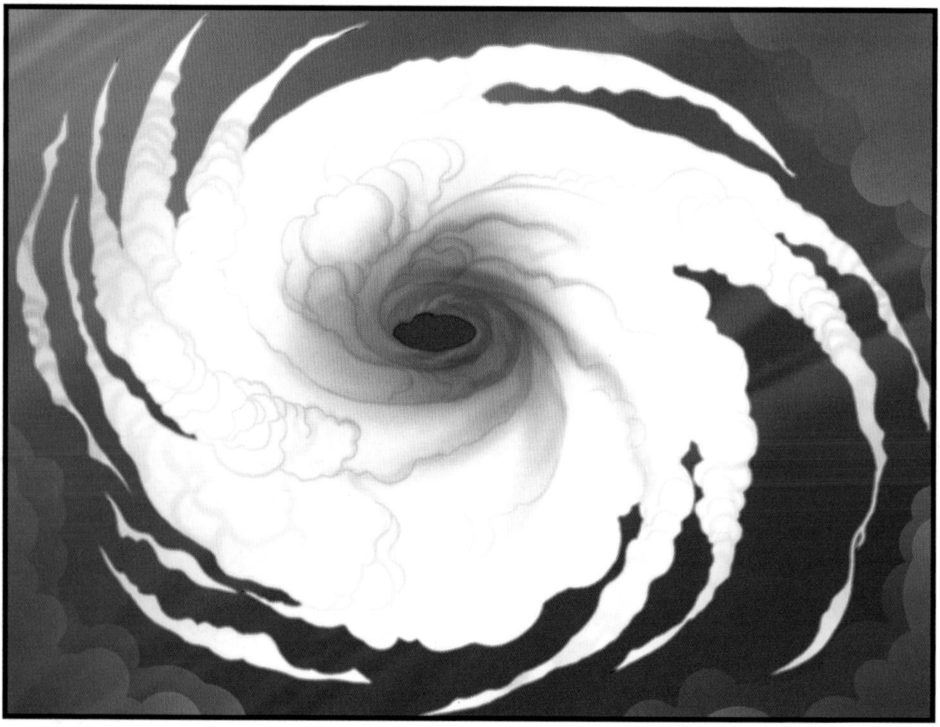

The hole in its center is the eye. The eye has calm winds.

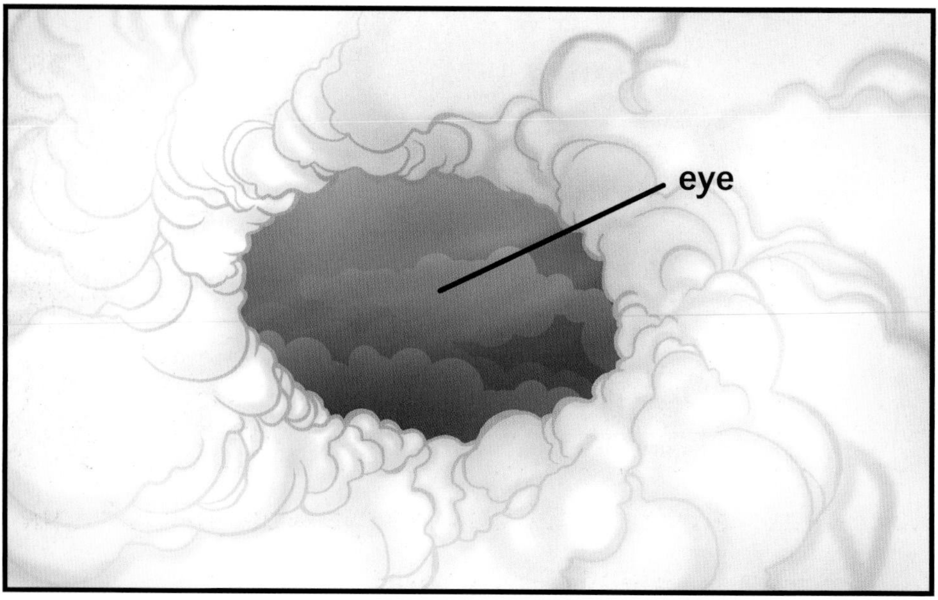
eye

The eye wall has the storm's most powerful winds.

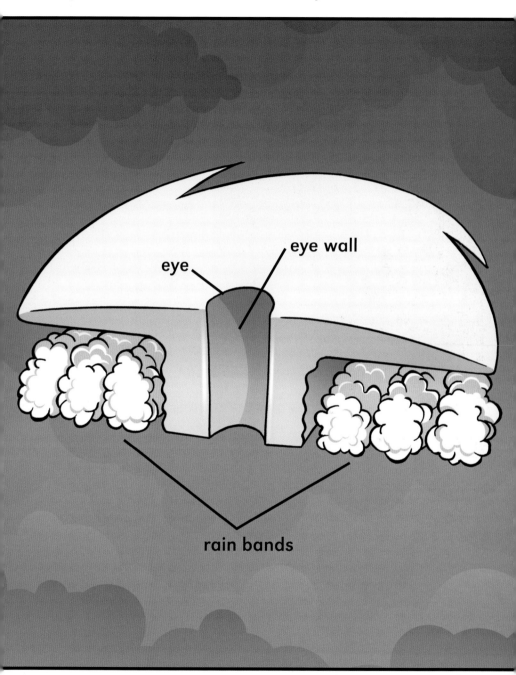

Rain bands stretch out from the eye wall. These bands carry heavy rain and strong winds.

Studying Hurricanes

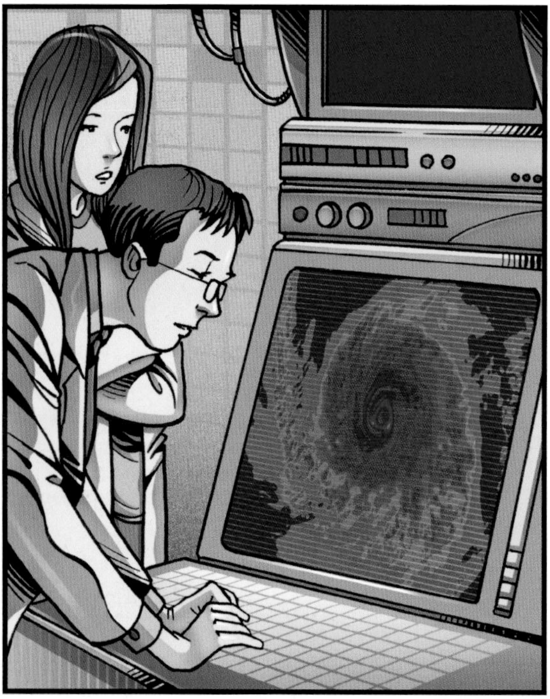

Scientists track hurricanes to predict their path and strength. They use tools to figure out where hurricanes might hit land.

Satellites take pictures of hurricanes from space.

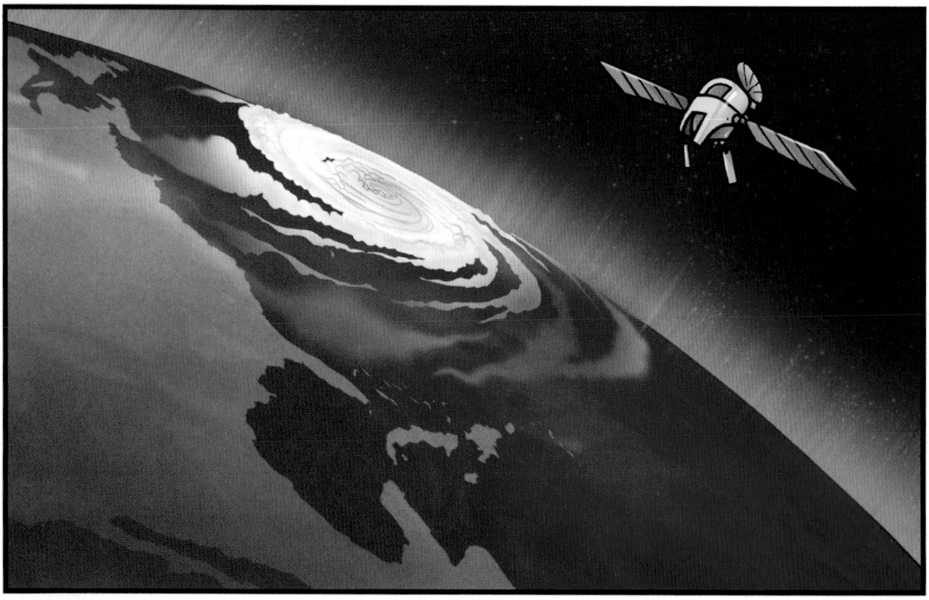

Planes fly into hurricanes to test wind speeds, temperature, and air pressure.

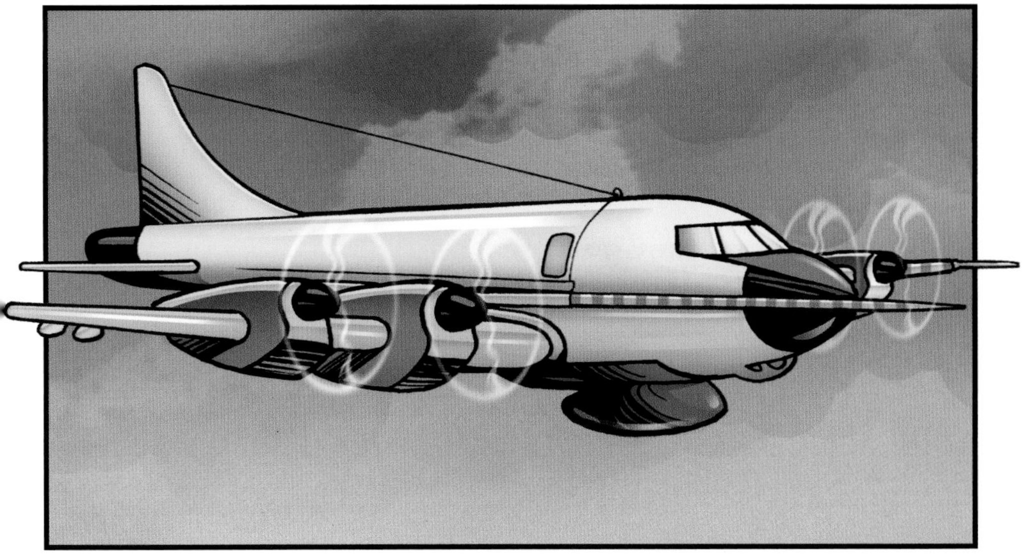

Scientists warn people when hurricanes are coming.

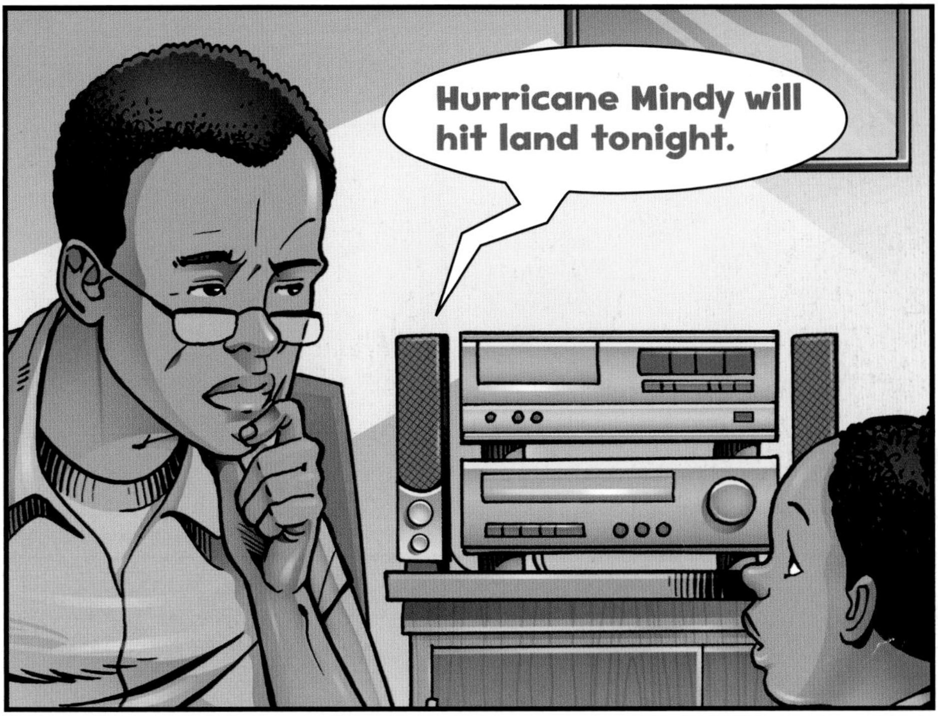
Hurricane Mindy will hit land tonight.

Scientists measure hurricane strength.

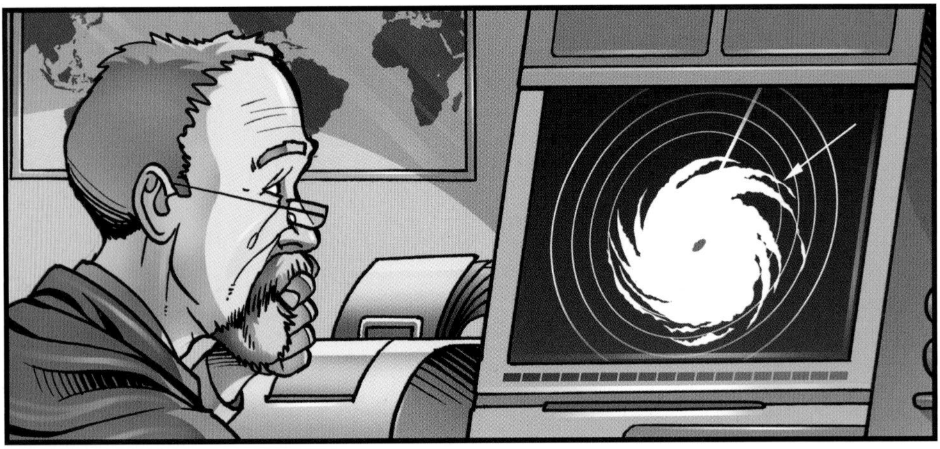

Weak hurricanes break tree branches and damage homes.

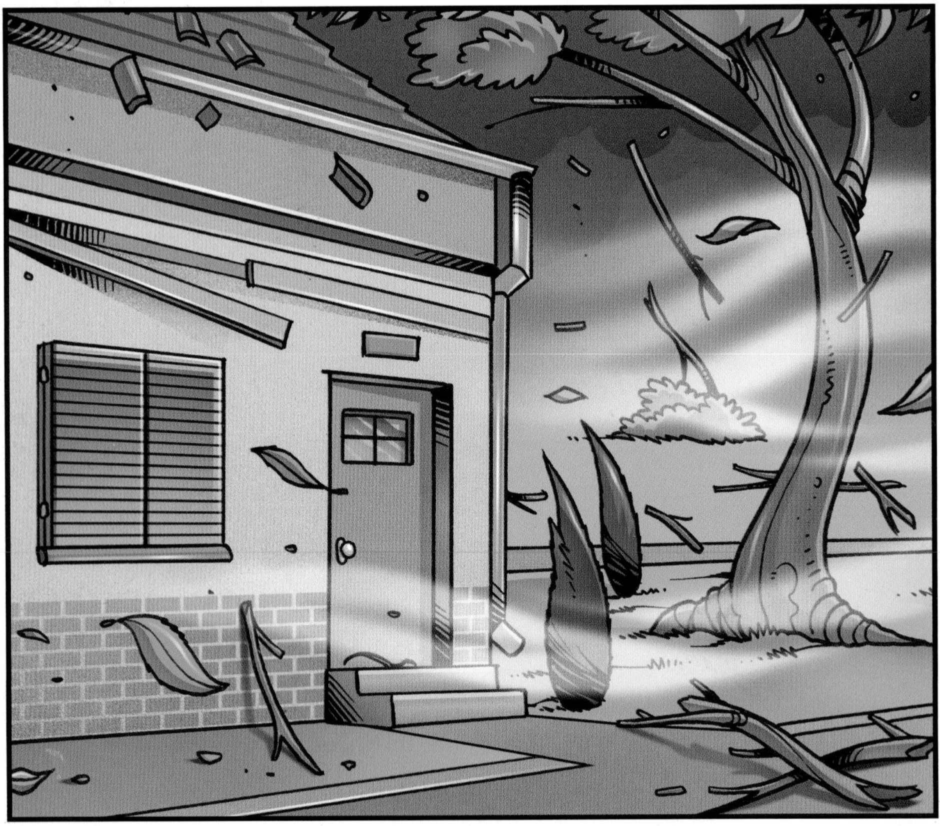

Strong hurricanes snap trees and destroy homes.

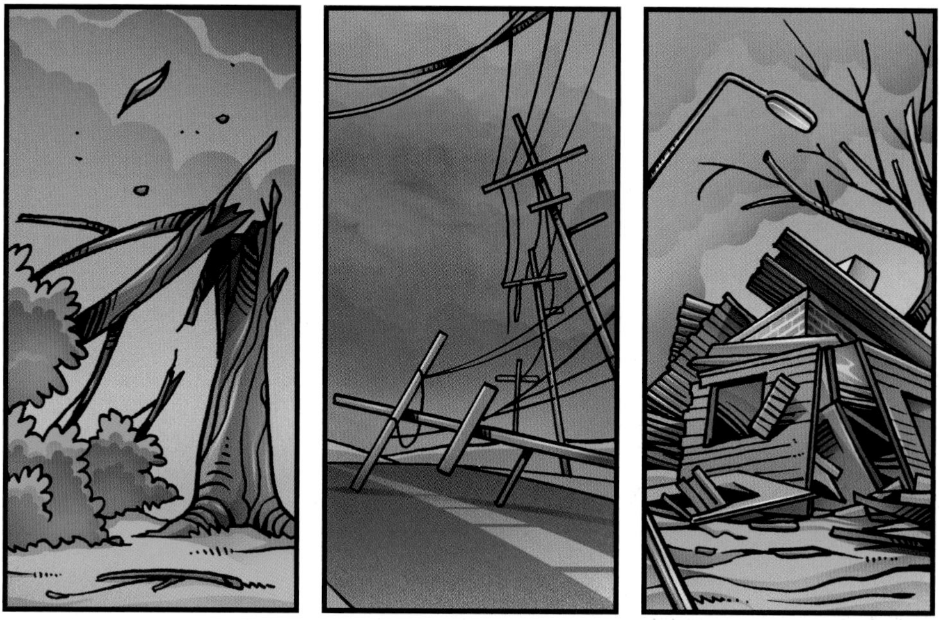

They also cause huge waves. These waves flood beaches and destroy homes near shore.

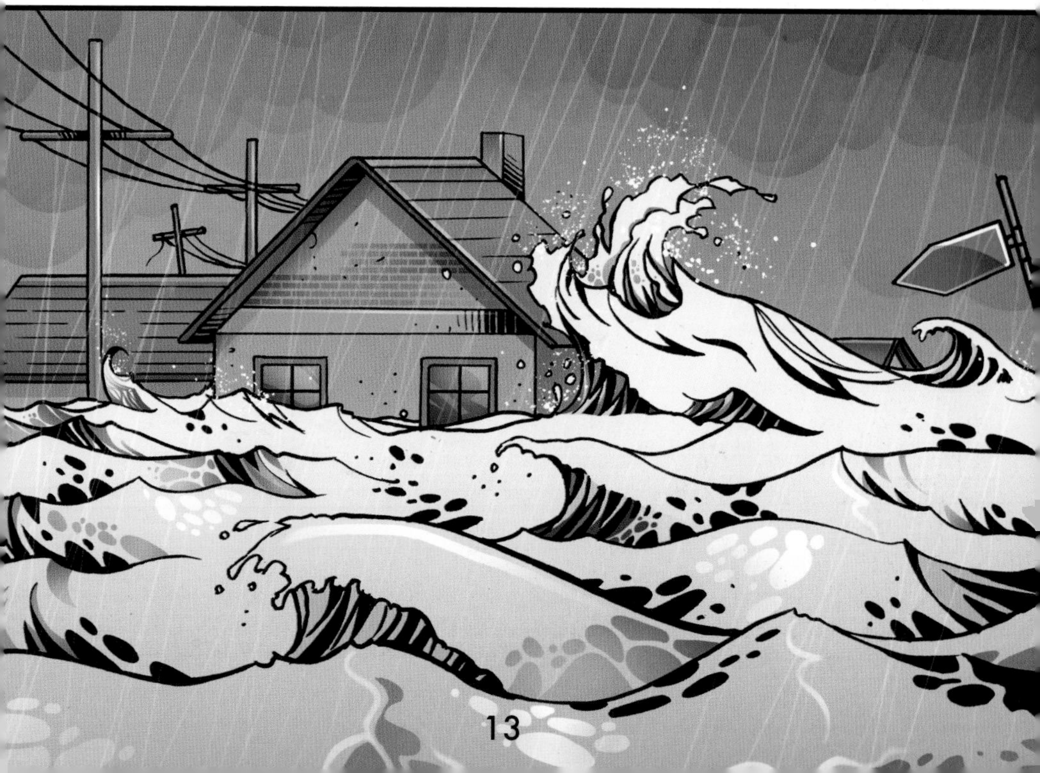

Sometimes more than one hurricane forms at a time.

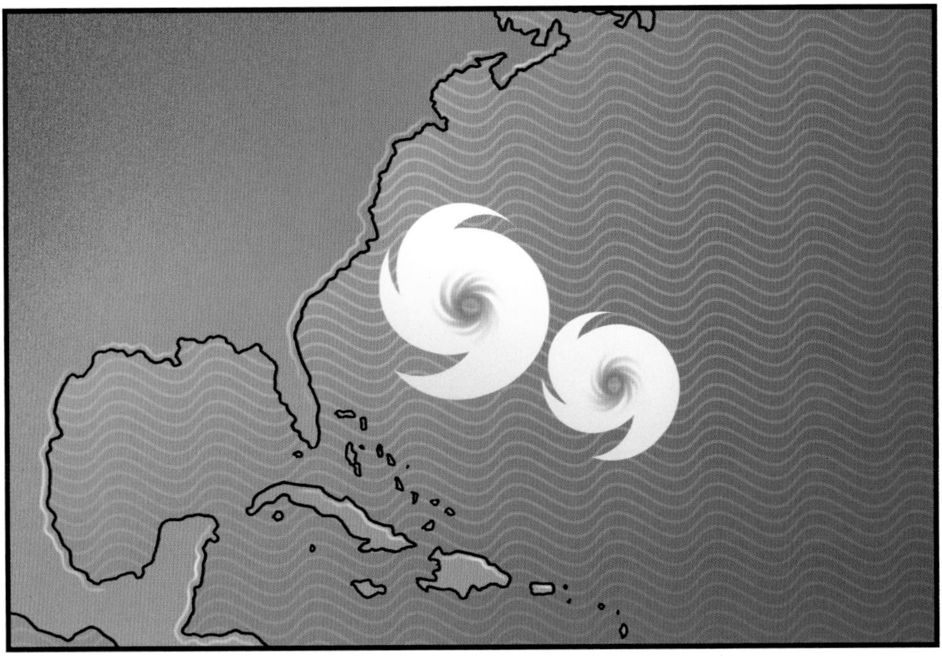

To track storms, all hurricanes are given names. The names switch between boy's and girl's names.

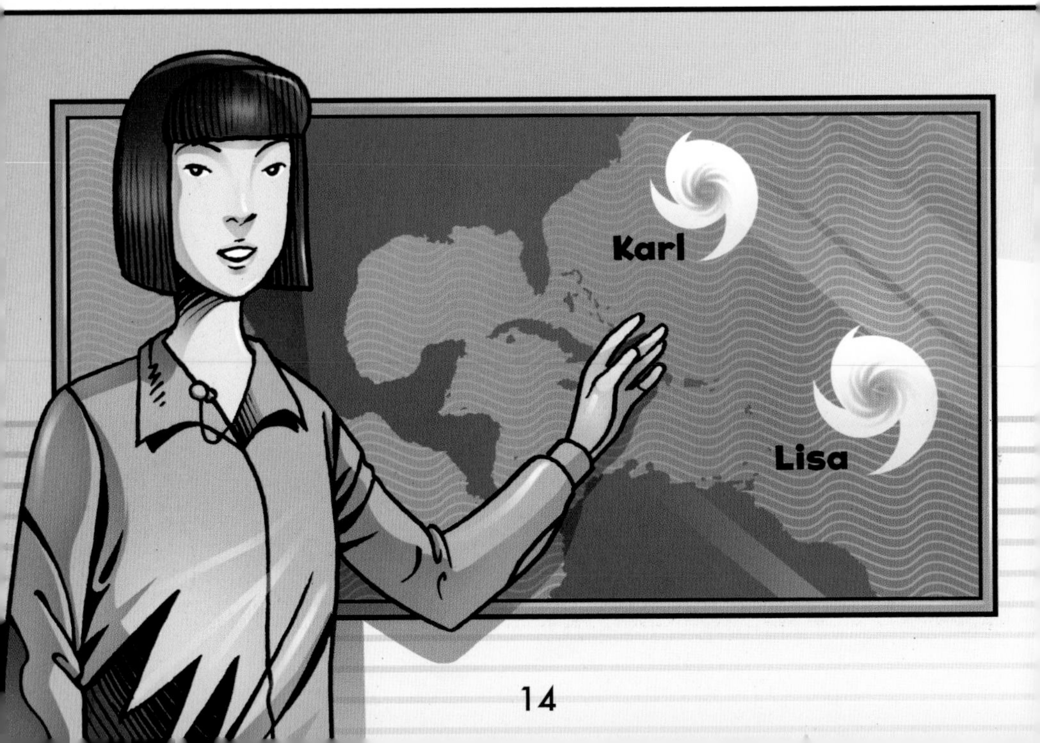
Karl
Lisa

The season's first hurricane begins with the letter A. Hurricane names follow the alphabet.

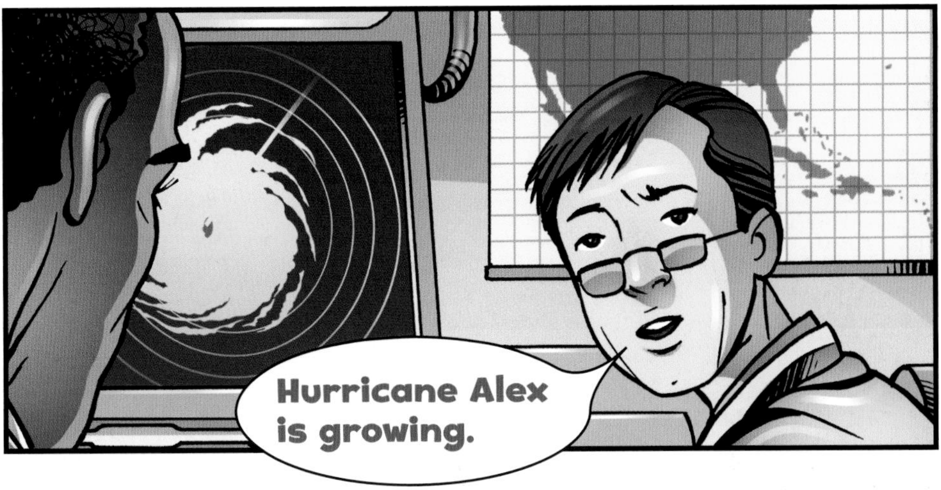
Hurricane Alex is growing.

Some hurricanes cause major damage. The names of these storms are never used again.

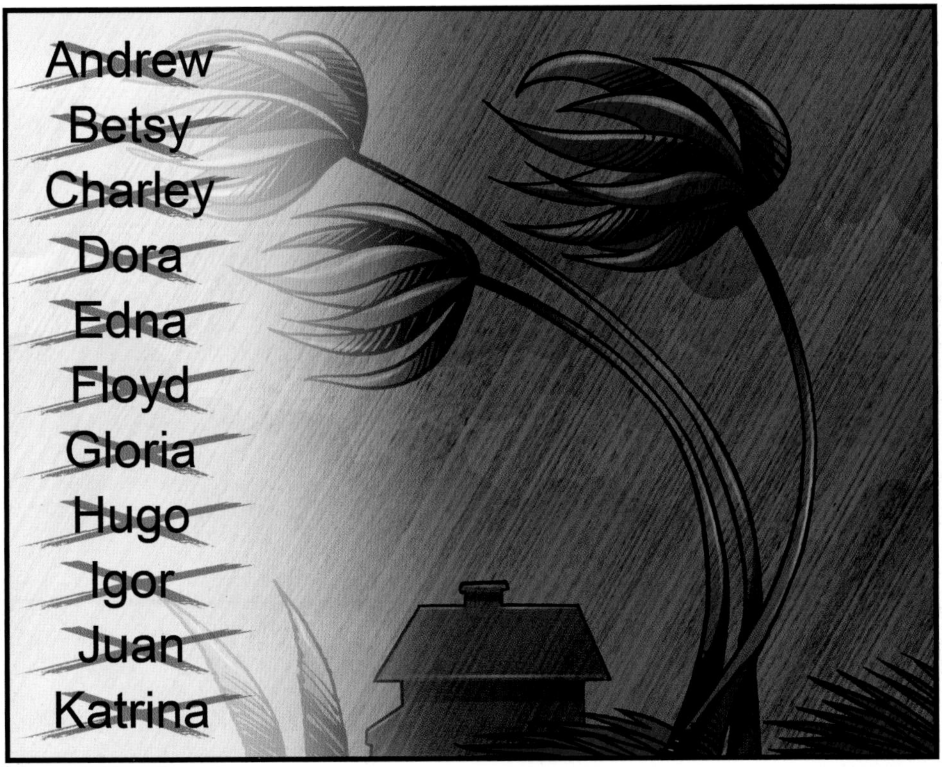
Andrew
Betsy
Charley
Dora
Edna
Floyd
Gloria
Hugo
Igor
Juan
Katrina

Staying Safe

Hurricanes don't strike without warning. Scientists track these storms days before they arrive.

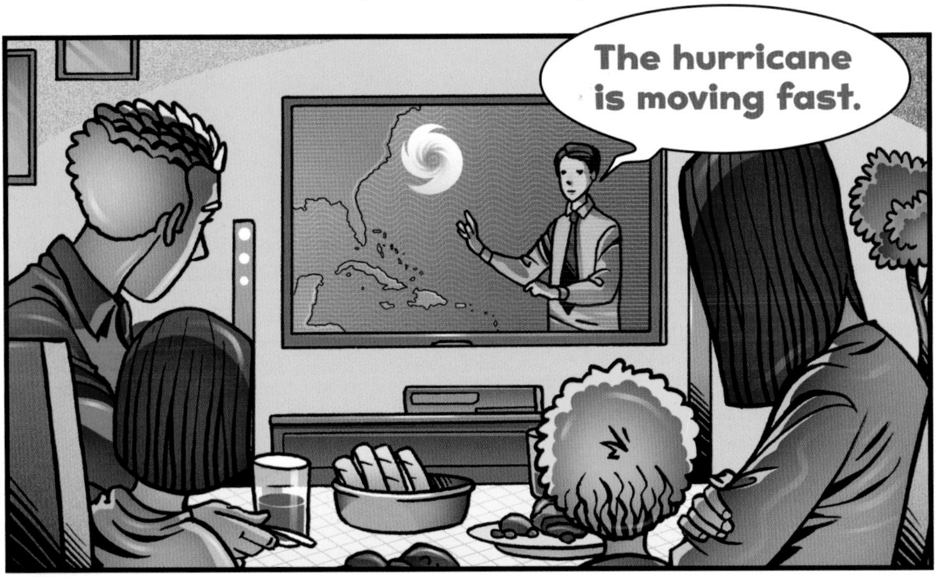
The hurricane is moving fast.

People near the coast need to prepare for the storm. They put away items that could blow away.

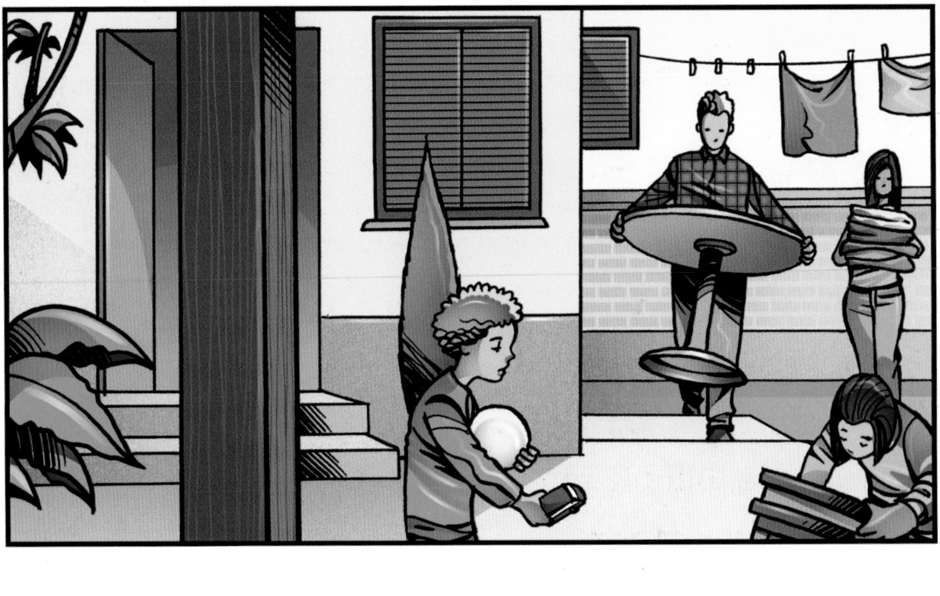

They board up windows so the glass doesn't break.

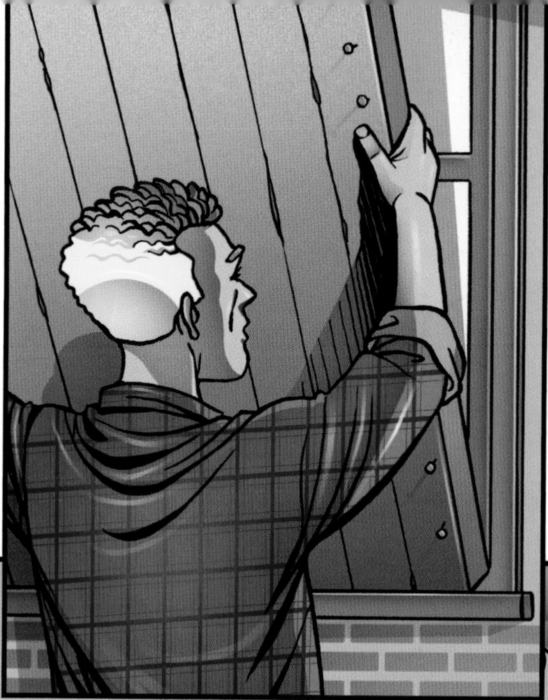

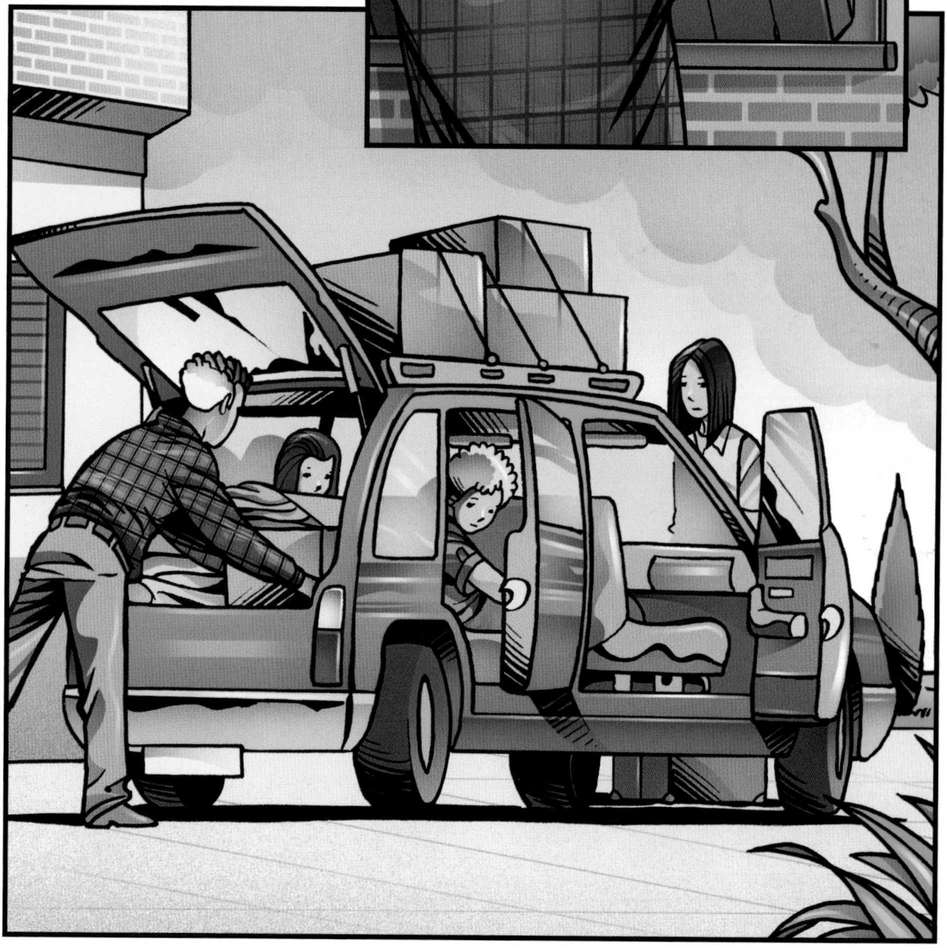

To stay safe, people may leave home to get farther away from the storm.

Hurricanes can knock out power for days. Pack an emergency kit for the storm.

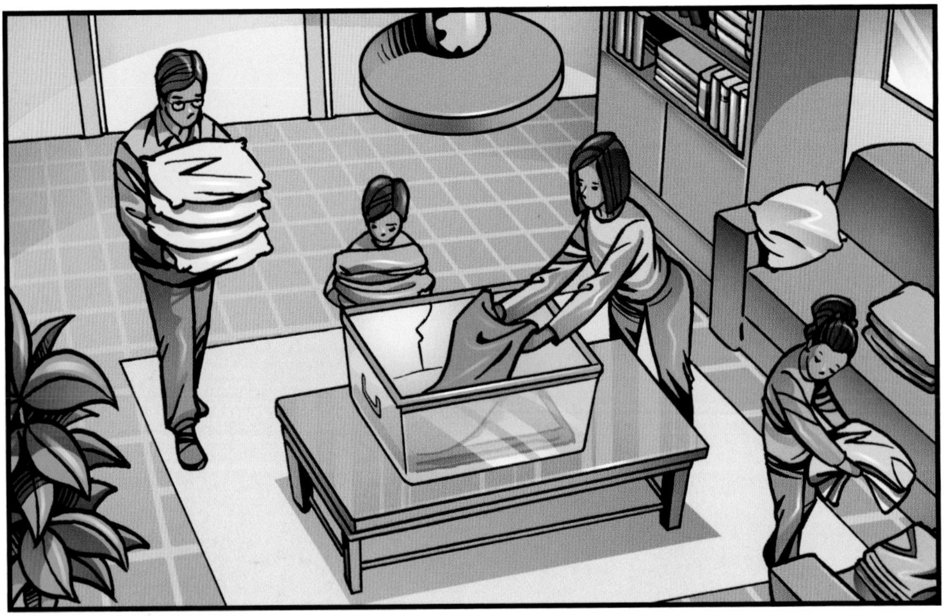

Keep a flashlight and a battery-powered radio nearby.

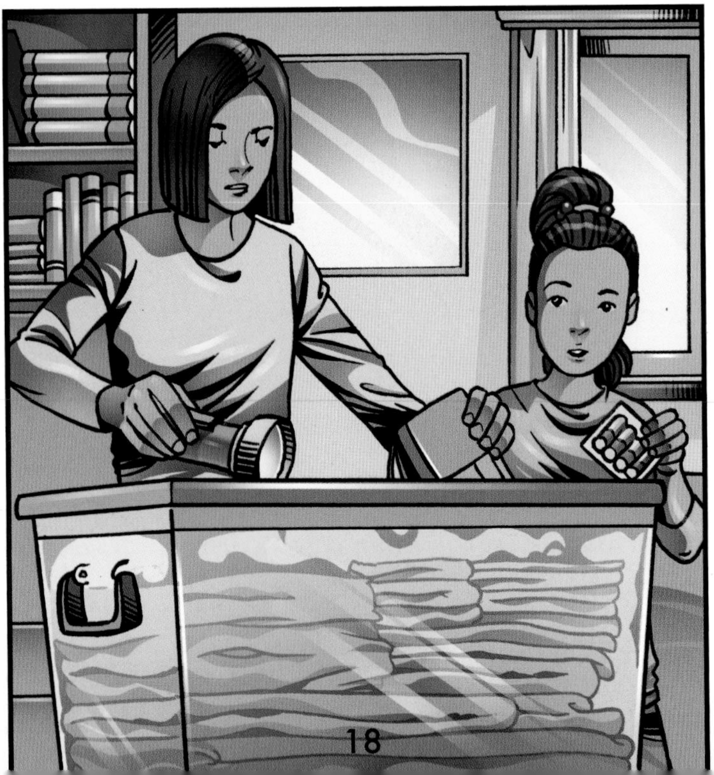

Have bandages and other first-aid supplies ready too.

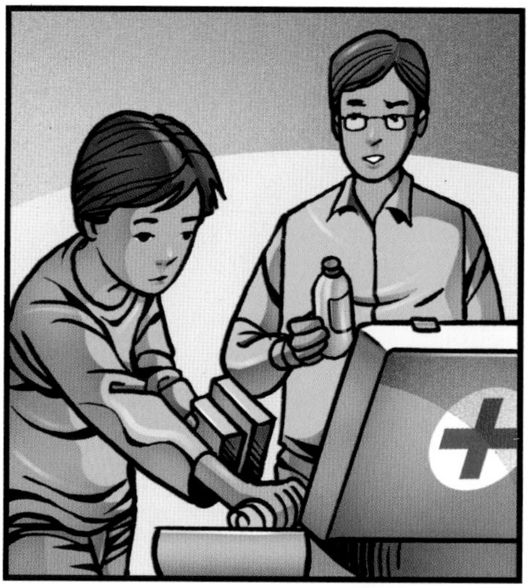

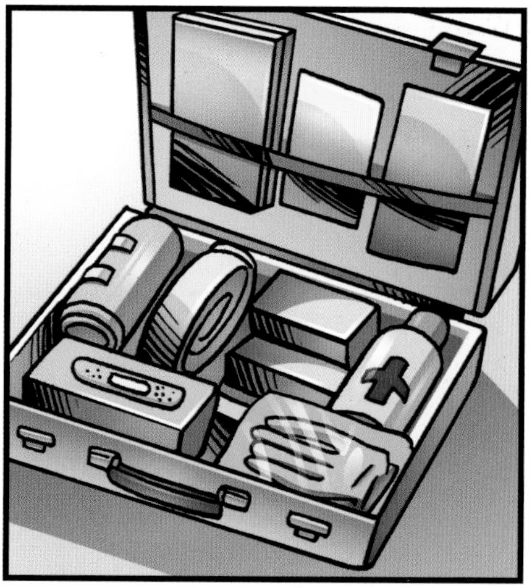

Stock shelves with bottled water and canned food.

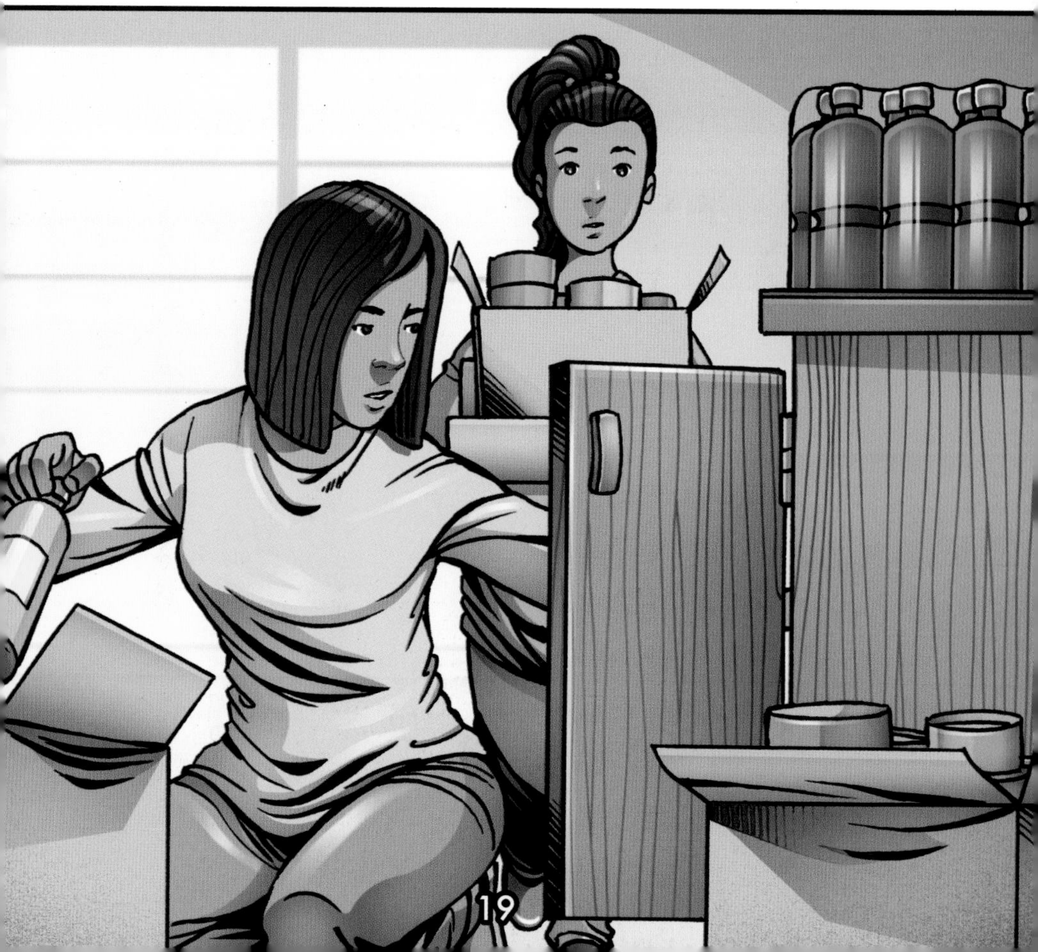

When a hurricane strikes, stay indoors.

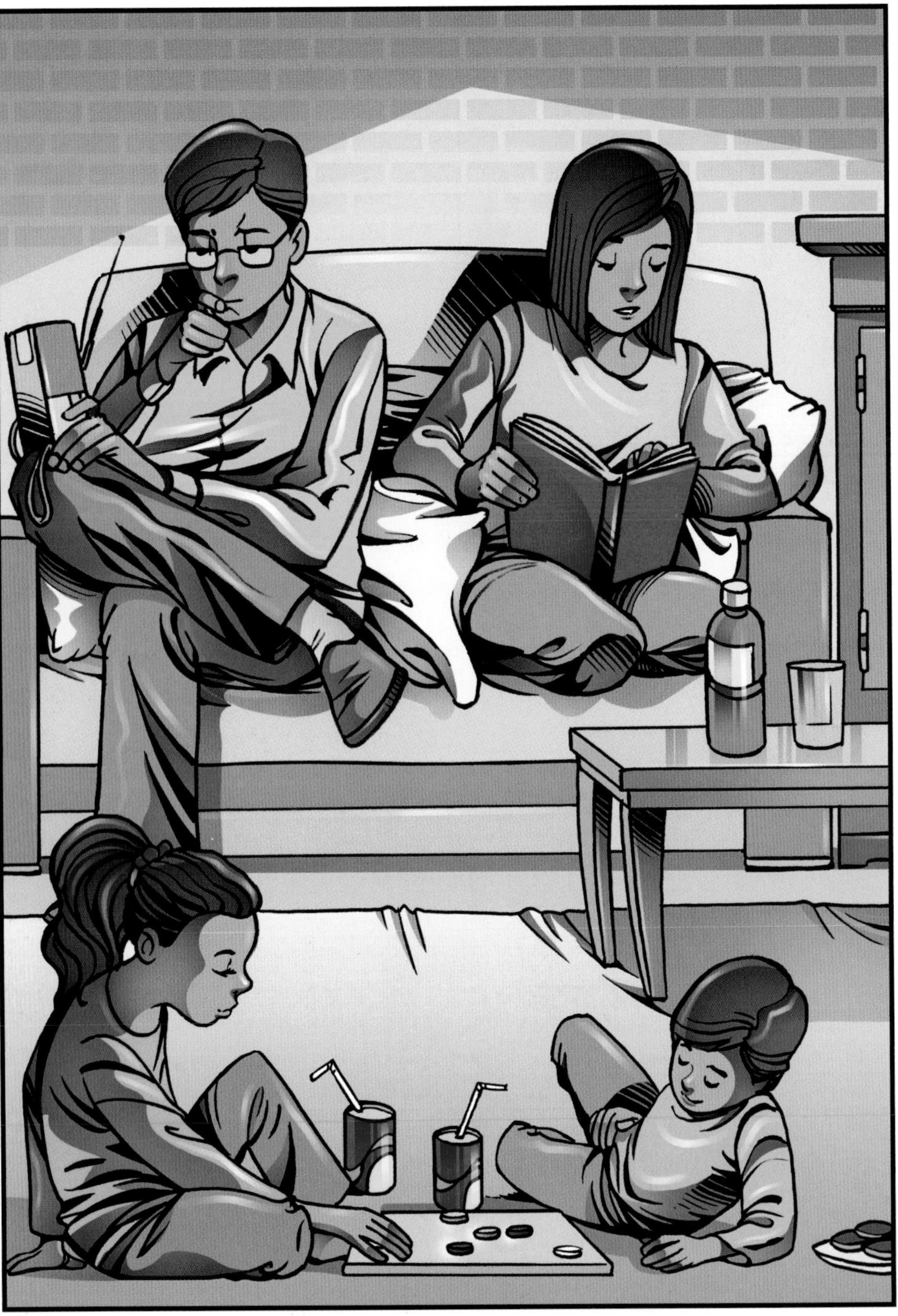

Keep away from windows and glass doors.

Listen to the radio for updates on the storm.

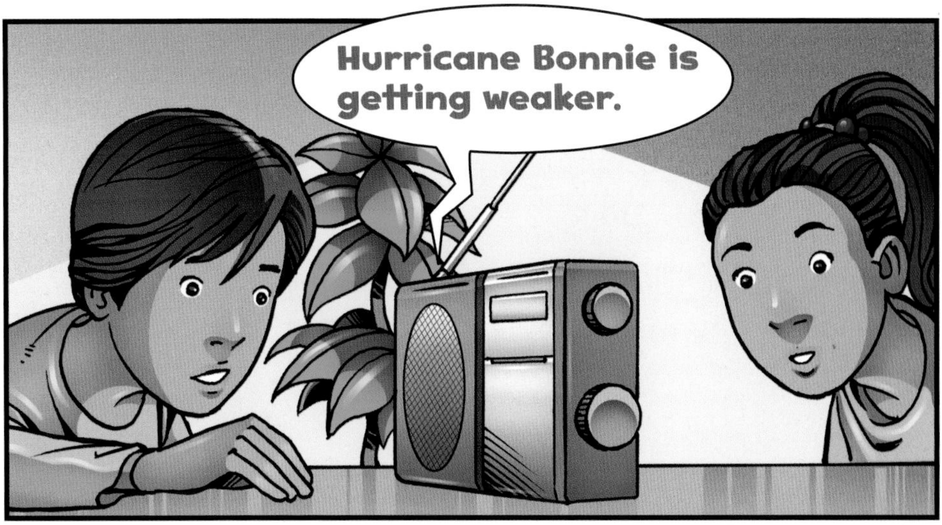
Hurricane Bonnie is getting weaker.

Knowing what to do during a hurricane helps you stay safe.

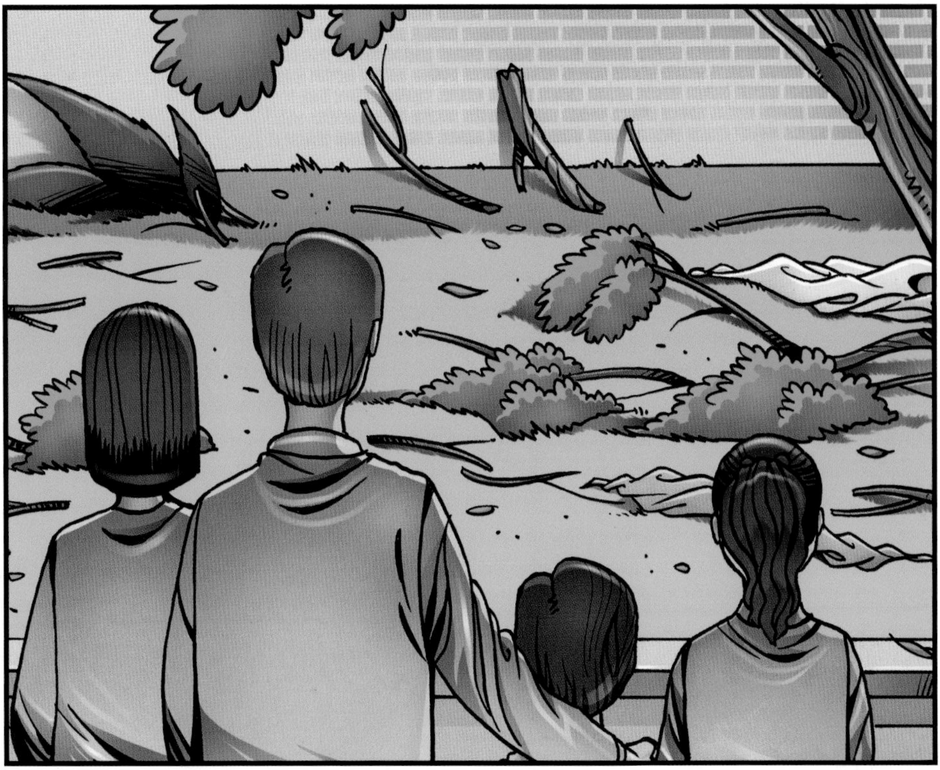

Glossary

air pressure—the weight of air pushing against something

eye wall—tall wall of fast-moving clouds lining the outer edge of a hurricane's eye

predict—to say what you think will happen in the future

rain bands—thunderstorms with heavy rain that spiral in toward the eye of a hurricane

satellite—a spacecraft that circles the earth; satellites gather and send information

track—to follow something

tropical—having to do with the hot and wet areas near the equator

Read More

Hawkins, John. *Hurricane Disasters.* Catastrophe! New York: Rosen Central, 2012.

Mezzanotte, Jim. *Hurricanes.* Wild Weather. Pleasantville, N.Y.: Weekly Reader, 2010.

Schuh, Mari. *Hurricanes.* Earth in Action. Mankato, Minn.: Capstone Press, 2010.

Internet Sites

FactHound offers a safe, fun way to find Internet sites related to this book. All of the sites on FactHound have been researched by our staff.

Here's all you do:

Visit *www.facthound.com*

Type in this code: 9781429676076

Super-cool stuff!

Check out projects, games and lots more at
www.capstonekids.com

Index

WILD EARTH

Titles in this Set:

EARTHQUAKES!

HURRICANES!

TORNADOES!

VOLCANOES!